# A CASE FOR
## *Skill*

Also by <sup>THE</sup>Life@Work Co.™

*A Case for Calling*
*A Case for Character*
*A Case for Serving*

THE Life@Work Co.™

# A CASE FOR
# *Skill*

*Discovering the Difference a Godly Man Makes in His Life at Work*

## DR. THOMAS ADDINGTON & DR. STEPHEN GRAVES

Cornerstone *Alliance*
FAYETTEVILLE, ARKANSAS 72702

Published by Cornerstone Alliance
Post Office Box 1928
Fayetteville, AR 72702

All Scripture quotations, unless otherwise indicated, are taken from the
HOLY BIBLE, NEW INTERNATIONAL VERSION®, NIV®.
Copyright © 1973, 1978, 1984 by International Bible Society. Used by
permission of Zondervan Publishing House. All rights reserved.

Scripture quotations cited as KJV are from the HOLY BIBLE, KING
JAMES VERSION.

ISBN 1-890581-04-6

Cover design by Sean Womack of Cornerstone Alliance.

Printed in the United States of America

1 3 5 7 9 10 8 6 4 2

*To our colleagues*

*the men and women*
*of Cornerstone Group*
*and Cornerstone Alliance*

*Thank you for living out*
*what this book describes.*

# *Series Introduction*

Our offices are on the fourth floor of the second tallest building in northwest Arkansas. We have an extraordinary view of the rolling hills of Fayetteville from our panoramic picture windows. Although our city is growing, it still has the feel of a small town. Almost everyone knows almost everyone.

From that vantage point we enjoy watching cycles of life unfold around us. Unlike some parts of the country, we benefit from the whole assortment of seasons. The snowy mantle of winter melts into the sweaty heat of summer, with all variations in between.

We also watch the daily routine of hundreds of businesses. At the start of a day we can see the lights of other businesses coming on, like eyes popping open after a good night's sleep. At the end of a day we witness those same lights going out. The next morning it begins all over again. Then again. Then again.

We talk to many men for whom that description sums up their work experience. People come and go; accounts open and close. Creditors get paid; customers get billed. We pick up; we deliver. We punch in; we punch out. The workday begins, then ends. We earn our money; we spend our money. The cycle is unrelenting and unending. Then the cycle quits, and we die.

Is that all there is? Is routine drudgery what a man should expect from his work life and career?

What is the difference in the behavior and experience of a Christian man in his work compared to that of a non-Christian man?

What does it mean to be a Christian who practices dentistry? Does it mean that I have Bible verses on my business card? Do I share Christ with patients while they are under anesthesia? Or perhaps I ought to treat only Christian patients. If someone doesn't pay me, should I send their bill into collections, or should I forgive the debt and maybe pay for it myself? Should I work longer hours to display an incredible work ethic? Or maybe I need to work shorter hours so that I can spend more time with my family or serve on a church or community committee. Do I pay my employees more than the national average? Or do I pay them less so they can learn to live by faith?

What does it mean to be a Christian plumber? Do I cut my rates for Christian customers? Should I work on Sunday, or do I fail to respond to a crisis that comes on the Sabbath? Perhaps I need to hand out gospel tracts to other subcontractors on the job. Should I release one of my crew if he's incompetent? Or are Christians bound to keep every employee on the payroll for life? What does the Bible say about work?

A number of years ago we came across a verse in the New Testament book of Acts that serves as God's final epitaph for King David:

> When David had served God's purpose in his own generation, he fell asleep. (Acts 13:36)

Those words complete a description of David found way back in the Old Testament book of Psalms:

> He chose David his servant and took him from the sheep pens; from tending the sheep he brought him to be the shepherd of his people Jacob, of Israel his inheritance. And David shepherded them with integrity of heart; with skillful hands he led them. (Psalm 78:70-72)

David was a shepherd, a musician, a soldier, and a king. He had a very busy, full, and successful career. We would like to use those verses about David as the basis for exploring the making of a godly man in and through his work world. This short series will consist of four parts:

....David... *served God's purpose...*:   A Case for Calling

He chose *David his servant...*:   A Case for Serving

....David shepherded them

with *integrity of heart*:   A Case for Character

....with *skillful hands* he led them:   A Case for Skill

So, we are back to one of our questions from above. Is work basically an unending and unfulfilling cycle of activity? Answer: it depends. On what? On whether or not I know God.

According to King Solomon, one of the wisest and wealthiest men of all time:

A man can do nothing better than to eat and drink and find satisfaction in his work. This too, I see, is from the hand of God.... *To the man who pleases him, God gives wisdom, knowledge and happiness, but to the sinner he gives the task of gathering and storing up wealth to hand it over to the one who pleases God.* (Ecclesiastes 2:24-26; italics added)

Without God in my life, I might be driven, full of ambition, and very successful. I might even make it to the pinnacle of my profession. But I will not enjoy my work over time. It will not bring me fulfillment. I will be on a treadmill.

These books address a Christian man in the workplace. The definition and clarity that the Bible brings to a man and his work world are reserved for those who enjoy a personal relationship with Jesus. If you don't know Him, we strongly urge you to invite Him into your life. Then join us in exploring the topic of work in the incredibly rich, amazingly untapped pages of Scripture.

May the favor of the Lord our God rest upon us;
establish the work of our hands for us—
yes, establish the work of our hands. (Psalm 90:17)

A word about our writing style. As coauthors, we speak in the first person when telling a story that relates to one of us as individuals. But we do not identify who belongs to which story. To help unravel that mystery, the following are some personal characteristics that will help sort us out.

Steve is an avid fisherman who baited hooks as a young boy on the Mississippi Gulf Coast. His appetite for learning and his energy for making friends have trademarked his twenty-three years of ministry and business.

Tom grew up in Hong Kong as the son of a medical missionary. He spent a number of years driving eighteen-wheelers, and he has taught at three universities.

We live in Fayetteville, Arkansas, love Scripture, and work together as business partners. Our companies and colleagues do work in organizational consulting and publishing. We have a passion to understand biblical principles that apply to work.

# *Book Introduction*

Skill is expected.

Of the four topics considered in this series, calling, serving, character, and skill, we probably know the least about skill. What does Scripture have to say about it?

Quite a bit, as it turns out. Skill is an incredibly rich concept in the Bible, in both the Old and New Testaments. In the Old Testament, God addresses skill directly and specifically with Moses when he is on Mount Sinai to transcribe the Ten Commandments.

One issue becomes very clear through this study. God expects skill in the work of His people. As Christians we do not have the option of mediocrity in our work.

Skill is expected.

# *Definition of Skill*

Understanding something completely
and transforming that knowledge
into creations of wonder
and excellence.

"And David shepherded them with integrity of heart; with
skillful hands he led them" (Psalm 78:72).

# CONTENTS

## CHAPTER ONE

## *What Is Skill?*

Bringing a 540,000-pound Boeing 747 onto the runway at Hong Kong's Kai Tak Airport is one of the ultimate tests of an airline pilot's skill. Professional pilots normally train on simulators that allow them to practice landings at almost every airport. Not so for most pilots flying into Hong Kong. Virtually every airline requires pilots to witness Hong Kong landings from a cockpit jump seat before they are allowed to land an airplane there on their own. According to Cathay Pacific pilot Bob Scott, Kai Tak Airport is as close as you can get in commercial aviation to making an aircraft-carrier landing. A former Royal Navy aircraft-carrier pilot, Scott contends, "If you can land in Hong Kong, then you can land just about anywhere."

Aviation experts maintain that no other final approach in the world is as complicated. The extremely mountainous terrain is supplemented by dense apartment blocks of housing that stretch almost to the very edge of the airport tarmac. The runway extends almost eleven thousand feet straight out into the Hong Kong harbor, on land reclaimed from the Pacific Ocean.

In roughly two minutes the aircraft drops from 1,800 to 675 feet. The landing gear is down, the flaps are extended, and the aircraft is screaming straight into a mountain. All of sudden, while the plane continues to descend, the pilot banks the aircraft as much as thirty degrees to the right in a 4,500-foot turn. Fifteen degrees is the most severe bank most passengers ever experience on a commercial flight. Pilots call it "The Turn." If you are on the right side of the airplane, you are looking directly into apartment windows. In the final thirty seconds of flight the pilot must level the airplane, center it on the runway, and touch down soon enough to avoid running into Victoria Harbor.

Captain Tom Overholt first flew into Hong Kong as a flight engineer on a Northwest Airlines 747. "I was working on the final checks. It was heavy weather; we broke out at just seven hundred feet. By the time I finished my job and swiveled my seat around, I couldn't believe it. I saw this mountain straight ahead and rooftops almost touching the wings. It took my breath away." Overholt calls it "the last real man's ride in the world."[1]

Growing up in Hong Kong, I lived two miles from the end of the runway, directly under the flight path. Landing lights for the final approach were on the roof of the two-story apartment building next to ours. It was against the law to fly kites because they could get tangled in the landing gear. A friend of mine with a good arm claimed he could hit airplanes with baseballs from our roof.

It was an awesome thing to see, hear, and feel those huge jets thunder overhead, just a few hundred feet off the ground. One right after another, they came in only minutes apart. No matter how many thousands I had already seen, I always had to watch the next one. The elite pilots who fly into Hong Kong are very good at what they do.

Skill in action is a wonderful thing to behold:

- A cardiac surgeon who displays confident dexterity in the process of repairing a defective heart valve.
- A professional truck driver who deftly maneuvers a fifty-five-foot eighteen-wheeler into a hard-to-get-to freight dock with only inches of leeway on either side.
- A tenacious salesman who negotiates through almost insurmountable obstacles to close a tough deal.

- A mechanic who finds and fixes a problem that no one else could find or fix.
- An artist who brings life in color out of a blank white canvas.
- A writer who arranges words to make a reader's blood boil, his heart laugh, or his brain think.

When we watch someone accomplish a task with skill, we are amazed. We say such things as "How did you do that?" "That was really something!" "Where did you learn to make that happen?" We love to see skill in action, but what is it exactly? What is skill, really?

### *The meaning of skill*

The Old Testament word for skill comes directly from the Hebrew word *to know*. But this *to know* does not indicate just a superficial understanding of something. It literally means to know completely and thoroughly, so that whatever can be known about something is known. It is the same word used in the King James Version of the Old Testament to describe sexual intimacy between a husband and a wife: "And Adam knew Eve his wife; and she conceived, and bare Cain" (Genesis 4:1, KJV). The word for skill describes knowing something intensely, exhaustively, and entirely. It means leaving nothing unexplored.

As if that were not enough, the definition goes even further. In addition to knowing something completely, skill also indicates the capacity to translate that knowledge into something of great value. According to Scripture, a skillful person is not just someone who has available a huge database of information should someone want to tap it. A person of skill is an individual who has a depth of understanding that is linked to an ability to take that knowledge and turn it into something of significant worth. Skill is often paired with words like *craftsman* and *fine workmanship*.

We attempt to capture the rich biblical meaning of skill as follows:

> Understanding something completely and transforming that knowledge into creations of wonder and excellence.

Frankly, this definition stunned us. We did not realize that Scripture talked much about skill at all, much less with this kind of vibrancy. We sat back from our study and could not help but reflect that the biblical level of skill is far away from where many, if not most, of us are in our work worlds. The implications are enormous.

## The usage of skill

Many of the words about skill in the Old Testament were used concerning the building of the tabernacle and the temple. Those two creations were perhaps more important to God then any other in the Old Testament era, apart from the actual work that He was doing in the hearts of His people. The tabernacle and then the temple were the primary dwelling places for God's presence. God was so concerned about the tabernacle's construction that He personally communicated the blueprint details to Moses. After He gave Moses the Ten Commandments, God held the prophet up on Mount Sinai for some additional and rather lengthy instruction, first regarding the furnishings of the tabernacle:

> Make the tabernacle with ten curtains of finely twisted linen and blue, purple and scarlet yarn, with cherubim worked into them by a *skilled craftsman.* (Exodus 26:1; italics added)

And again a few verses later: "Make a curtain of blue, purple and scarlet yarn and finely twisted linen, with cherubim worked into it by a *skilled craftsman*" (Exodus 26:31; italics added).

Then, the focus shifts to the uniform of the priest while he is in the tabernacle: "Tell all the *skilled men* to whom I have given wisdom in such matters that they are to make garments for Aaron, for his consecration, so he may serve me as priest" (Exodus 28:3; italics added). Then, "Fashion a breastpiece for making decisions—the work of a *skilled craftsman*" (Exodus 28:15; italics added)

But the most fascinating reference is the following one, in which God identifies with great precision the craftsmen He has in mind for the project:

Then the Lord said to Moses, "See, I have chosen Bezalel son of Uri, the son of Hur, of the tribe of Judah, and I have filled him with the Spirit of God, with *skill, ability and knowledge in all kinds of crafts*—to make artistic designs for work in gold, silver and bronze, to cut and set stones, to work in wood, and to engage in all kinds of craftsmanship. Moreover, I have appointed Oholiab son of Ahisamach, of the tribe of Dan, to help him. Also *I have given skill to all the crafts-men* to make everything I have commanded you: the

Tent of Meeting, the ark of the Testimony with the atonement cover on it, and all the other furnishings of the tent—the table and its articles, the pure gold lampstand and all its accessories, the altar of incense, the altar of burnt offering and all its utensils, the basin with its stand—and also the woven garments, both the sacred garments for Aaron the priest and the garments for his sons when they serve as priests, and the anointing oil and fragrant incense for the Holy Place. They are to make them just as I commanded you." (Exodus 31:1-11; italics added)

God Himself took such an intense personal interest in setting the standard for skill at the highest level. Of all of the things He chose to talk about up on that mountain with Moses, a significant portion of communication dealt with skilled craftsmen—sometimes by name. God did not have only a passing, casual interest in skill. Far from it—He was directly involved in describing it, identifying it, and giving direction to it.

Throughout Scripture, the word *skill* is applied to a host of different careers, such as writers, traders, musicians, loggers, leaders, weavers, speakers, soldiers, and metalworkers, to mention a few. There can be no question from the usage of the word that skill is very close to the center of God's attention and His heart.

With that in mind, it is not at all surprising that David, a man after God's own heart, was identified by God as a skilled leader. Neither should it be astonishing that Solomon observes in Proverbs: "Do you see a man skilled in his work? He will serve before kings; he will not serve before obscure men" (Proverbs 22:29).

If skill is something worthy of the King's personal attention, then certainly it will be noticed and appreciated by a king.

## CHAPTER TWO

# *Raising the Skill Level*

A good friend of ours worked for years in a Fortune 50 company. Mike (not his real name) signed on as a young college graduate and moved up through the ranks rather quickly. He was skilled in information systems as well as marketing, and he held a variety of assignments as his career progressed. Mike worked for five years before he met a Christian who was known in the company for his level of skill.

Until he met another Christian (we will call him Todd), Mike did not advertise widely that he was a follower of Jesus. Why? Because he was afraid of persecution? No. Because he was ashamed to be identified with Christ? No. Because as a whole, his Christian coworkers did not distinguish themselves with high levels of competence.

The Christians in the organization had a great reputation for showing stellar character and for being wonderful servants. They had Scripture verses on their desks. They conducted Bibles studies during lunch breaks. They helped colleagues navigate personal problems. They did not steal company technology or cash. They were very open about their faith. Everybody trusted them. And it was not so much that they were bad at what they did. They just were not very good at what they did.

But Mike kept hearing about Todd. Todd was an aggressive Christian. No one who worked with and for him was uncertain about Whom he served and what he believed. But make no mistake. He was also at the top of his game. In an extremely competitive corporate environment, this man was viewed both inside and outside the company as one of the best in the world at what he did. He was on the cutting edge of a technology that he had helped develop and that he continued to improve. He often received calls from top executives of noncompeting companies around the world who wanted to learn from him. In one case we know about, a board chairman flew his entire board on two corporate Gulfstream IVs to spend two days with Todd.

Like loads of other folks in the company, Mike wanted to work for Todd. So he kept putting in for assignments to work with this fellow and eventually was transferred to the team that Todd led. For Mike, it was like a cup of cool water on a hot day—to work for an overt Christian who was extraordinarily skilled at what he did. That man became Mike's mentor and still occupies that role today.

### *God's definition of skill raises the standard.*

The definition of skill that comes out of Scripture is worlds away from work defined by mediocrity. Skill in the Bible is not the characteristic of someone who says, "I guess I know enough to get by" or "I suppose I'm doing an OK job because I'm still receiving a paycheck." A person of skill does not excuse his mediocre work with such words as "I've been here twenty-five years, so I ought to get some respect from people around here." The skill of Scripture is the kind of quality that knows something better, understands something more thoroughly, and translates something more completely into a creation of unique worth than anything else could.

Our ultimate example of skill is embodied in the life that Jesus lived on this earth. He healed in cases where no other physician could make disease go away. He was persuasive even with Pharisees and doctors of the law, who had an obvious agenda to get rid of Him. Jesus mentored His disciples so well that after His ascension into heaven they took the Good News around the world. There was virtually nothing Jesus did during the three-plus years of His full-time ministry that did not demonstrate great skill.

But He also was very skilled as a carpenter before those years of full-time ministry. The word used to describe Jesus in Mark 6:3 is the Greek word *tekton*. As William Barclay notes, "A *tekton* was more than a carpenter; he was a craftsman who could build a wall or a house, construct a boat, or make a table or a chair, or throw a bridge across a little stream."[1] Even before He was publicly identified as the Messiah, Jesus was known as a skilled craftsman. *Tekton* pictures someone who, with a minimum of technical equipment and a maximum of craftsmanship, could make something of beauty out of very little.

In many of the older cities of Europe it was common for craftsmen to hang a sign outside their shop that indicated their trade and their slogan. It was the same in Israel during New Testament times. In Matthew 11:30, Jesus commented that His yoke is easy. The Greek word for *easy* means "well-fitting." Perhaps the sign that hung above the door of His carpenter's shop in Nazareth was in the form of an ox yoke with the words "My yokes fit well" inscribed on it.[2]

## Speed vs. quality

Sometime during the Industrial Revolution a subtle shift began to take place in the crafts. Speed and uniformity eventually became more important than quality and craftsmanship. A craftsman was someone who understood his specific craft from start to finish. The advent of the assembly line divided the process of making something into small parts. An assembly-line worker does not know and understand the entire creation process for a product. He only knows his small fragment.

It has only been in the last few years that the spotlight has turned back to quality. The Total Quality movement attempts to take a craftsmanlike approach within the context of high-speed manufacturing. Zero defects is the goal—proper engineering before the process begins. Every worker in the process becomes responsible for the quality of the final product. Inspection of raw materials occurs on the front end instead of inspection of finished product on the back end.

We do not at all suggest that the Industrial Revolution, the assembly line, and all the progress they have contributed are bad. But we do know this for sure: Regardless of the context of my work, the Bible makes it clear that I am to bring skill to the task. I bring a craftsman's eye and intensity to what I am doing.

I can do that in any environment, even if it is not expected or rewarded.

## CREDENTIALS VS. COMPETENCE

We love credentials. Degrees. Certifications. Awards. Undergraduate education. Graduate school. Postgraduate work. They may all be part of contributing to a person's level of skill. But they are not the same thing as skill. And in some cases they do not bring much to the table at all.

According to Scripture, skill consists of a combination of

1. Raw ability, which comes directly from God;
2. Filling by the Holy Spirit in specific relation to the task He wants me to accomplish; and
3. Experience, education, and maturity in combination with each other.

When I taught at the university, students often came to me and asked if I thought they ought to continue for more advanced degrees. After we sat down and mapped out what they wanted to accomplish once they left the academic environment, it was often clear whether or not more education would be helpful. In many cases it was. In at least as many situations, however, an additional credential probably would not have been helpful.

Credentials do not by themselves create a skilled man. They can, however, be part of an indispensable package that aids him in becoming a man of skill.

So if I'm a Christian, how should I look on the job? Do I have an option to be mediocre? Is it OK just to be OK? Should I be happy with a slightly above average performance review? Should I be content to let other people in the company carry the brunt of being able to make things happen?

Obviously not. Scripture sets a higher standard for my competence level at work than anything else we have ever been exposed to. As a Christian in the workplace, I ought to have an insatiable curiosity to learn what I need to know to understand my work thoroughly and to the core. There should be no question around the office, on the job, or in the company about my level of skill.

The word *Christian* should be synonymous with words like *wonder* and *excellence*.

### The Holy Spirit lifts our level of skill.

I understand the Holy Spirit's role in calling. How can I know my calling unless He communicates it to me? I understand the Holy Spirit's role in character. It is virtually impossible to develop godly character without the Holy Spirit. I also understand the Holy Spirit's role in serving. How can I learn how to be a good servant without His help in my life?

But what is the Holy Spirit's role in skill? Far more significant that any of us might have thought.

As we mentioned before, while Moses was up on the mountain receiving the Ten Commandments and other instructions directly from the mouth of God, one of the most surprising things God said related to specific men and their skill. God identified Bezalel as a skilled man whom He wanted directly involved in the tabernacle project. That by itself is amazing. But there is more to the equation in this case. Bezalel was not only specifically chosen by God for a task, the man was also filled with the Holy Spirit for that task: "I have chosen Bezalel . . . and I have filled him with the Spirit of God . . . for work" (Exodus 31:2-4).

Bezalel as a skilled craftsman was personally appointed by God. Then he was filled with the Holy Spirit specifically as a supplement to his skill as a craftsman, for the purpose of his work.

Moses then confirmed that combination of skill and God's Spirit when announcing Bezalel's appointment to the nation of Israel in Exodus 35.

> Then Moses said to the Israelites, "See, the Lord has chosen Bezalel son of Uri, the son of Hur, of the tribe of Judah, and he *has filled him with the Spirit of God,* with skill, ability and knowledge in all kinds of crafts—to make artistic designs for work in gold, silver and bronze, to cut and set stones, *to work* in wood and to engage in all kinds of artistic craftsmanship." (Exodus 35:30-33; italics added)

But Bezalel is far from unique. Later as Moses was struggling to accomplish all his duties as leader of God's people, the Holy Spirit was given to a group of men designated to help him. Moses did not have time to arbitrate between all the disputes of the Israelite nation. So he appointed seventy elders who could judge the easier cases and leave only the most difficult ones for himself. As that responsibility was given to the elders:

> The Lord said to Moses: "Bring me seventy of Israel's elders who are known to you as leaders and officials

among the people. Have them come to the Tent of
Meeting, that they may stand there with you. I will
come down and speak with you there, and I will take
of the Spirit that is on you and put the Spirit on them.
They will help you carry the burden of the people so
that you will not have to carry it alone." (Numbers
11:16-17)

In the book of Judges, there is a whole string of leaders for
whom the Holy Spirit and their call to a specific work task
came simultaneously:

- Othniel in Judges 3:10;
- Gideon in Judges 6:34;
- Jephthah in Judges 11:29; and
- Samson in Judges 13:25.

David was filled with God's Spirit at the time of his anointing as king of Israel in 1 Samuel 16:13.

In the New Testament the disciples were given the task of
carrying the gospel all over the world. That great commission
was specifically linked with the coming of the Holy Spirit to
help them fulfill that task: "But you will receive power when
the Holy Spirit comes on you; and you will be my witnesses in

Jerusalem, and in all Judea and Samaria, and to the ends of the earth" (Acts 1:8).

Those are just a few examples from Scripture that link the work that we are to do and the filling that the Holy Spirit gives us. Our passion for Jesus and the role of the Holy Spirit in our lives are not limited only to being a "great dad." Or developing our character. Or even staying sexually pure. Our passion for Jesus is just as relevant and just as necessary when it comes to the skill that we bring to our work.

The work of the Holy Spirit in our work life is a crucial distinguishing mark in accomplishing tasks on the job. The non-Christian has raw ability that God gives. The non-Christian also has the benefit of education, experience, and maturity. But the non-Christian does not have the Spirit of God as part of his work equation. One out of three very important ingredients is missing. The Holy Spirit plays an indispensable role in lifting our level of skill.

## CHAPTER THREE

## *Getting Focused*

Bill McCartney, cofounder of Promise Keepers, is as focused a man as we have ever met. He is intense. He is passionate. There is very little he does not observe. When you have a conversation with him, he looks right through you and goes to the core. There is not much small talk with Coach.

Part of that is a result of his personality. That is the kind of guy he is. We did not know him when he was a college football coach, but his players would probably describe him in somewhat the same way.

But there is more to his focus than just his personality. He is in a second career. Among other things, that means he is developing a new set of skills that relate specifically to God's new calling on his life.

As CEO of Promise Keepers, he is constantly pulled in different directions and into diverse situations, both from inside and outside the organization. But he will not allow himself to be pulled anywhere that does not conform to the skill set that God has given him and that he is developing. At the same time, he is drawn like a magnet to areas to which he feels called and which are aligned with his skill.

**Focus.** You just do not meet great leaders who have a scattered focus. Good leaders know what they are all about. They concentrate in areas where their skills are best utilized and where those skills shine.

That strategy and orientation come right out of Scripture.

### Developing skill requires focus.

**Solomon.** When Solomon took over the throne from his father, David, as the king of Israel, he spent some quiet time with God. Solomon had already established that he would follow in the footsteps of his father, David. According to the text, he showed his love for God by walking according to the statutes his father had lived by.

During an encounter with God at the very beginning of Solomon's reign, God appeared to him and told him to ask for whatever he wanted God to give him. Solomon responded very simply: "Give your servant a discerning heart to govern your people and to distinguish between right and wrong" (1 Kings 3:9).

Just one focused sentence of request! Solomon didn't have a grocery list. As a young king, burdened with the kinds of judgments and decisions that he would have to make, he focused on a specific kind of skill that would make him a good king.

To this day, Solomon is known as a wise man. According to Scripture, he was the wisest man who ever lived, except for Jesus Christ. The Old Testament books that he authored, Song of Solomon and Proverbs, are referred to as "wisdom literature."

If you had gone to Solomon and asked the question, "What skill do you need to develop in order to do your job well?" he could have answered on the spot, "I need a discerning heart to govern my people and to distinguish between right and wrong." For Solomon, his entire ability to govern well came down to that one statement. He could articulate it; he focused on it; he wrote about it; and he asked God for it. It is the skill that distinguished him from other kings.

Solomon's skill in these matters did not come entirely with one sweep of God's hand over him. The fact that Solomon had skill implied that he had been a diligent student of God's Word, of nature, of his father's method of ruling the kingdom, and of other disciplines of learning. God does not seem to endow someone with skills who is not actively pursuing them on a natural plane.

Developing an exceptionally focused sense of what I do does not mean that I cannot have a wide range of interests. Look at Solomon. He was an incredible businessman. Scripture contends that Solomon was wealthier than any man who has ever lived before or since. He could negotiate, and he could trade. Furthermore, he understood a wide range of knowledge beyond governing. Ecclesiastes discourses about pleasure and work, leadership and knowledge, as well as wisdom. The range of subjects that Solomon writes about in Proverbs is truly remarkable.

**Paul.** In much the same way as Solomon, Paul brought a focused skill to his work. We know precisely what his calling was. God told Ananias, "This man [Paul] is my chosen instrument to carry my name before the Gentiles and their kings and before the people of Israel" (Acts 9:15). Paul himself confirmed that calling when he reported to the Galatians what the apostles had concluded about his mission: "They saw that I had been entrusted with the task of preaching the gospel to the Gentiles, just as Peter had been to the Jews" (Galatians 2:7).

We also know that Paul was filled with the Holy Spirit when Ananias laid hands on him. But what was the focus of his skill?

Paul developed a magnificent skill in communicating Christ persuasively in multiple contexts and cultures. Consider some examples:

- *To Jewish Christians.* The Jerusalem Council, which is described in Acts 15, dealt with a volatile issue that was very traumatic to the early church. Should Gentile believers be required to undergo circumcision? Paul, along with Peter, Barnabas, and James, convinced the apostles and elders not to place that added burden on new Gentile believers.

- *To Greek philosophers.* Acts 17 records one of the most complete and remarkable speeches in all the Bible. Paul grabbed an opportunity to speak to a group of Epicurean and Stoic philosophers at the Areopagus, which was their place of discussion and debate. He presented the gospel, using their own beliefs and per-suasive communication techniques to his advantage. He knew the Greek culture and its prevailing thought so well that some of the philosophers who listened actually became followers of Christ.

- *To local churches.* Paul planted churches and spoke in more than thirty locations across Palestine, Asia, Macedonia, and Italy. He also wrote a series of letters, which we still enjoy as thirteen of our New Testament books.

- *To Roman rulers.* Paul was able to convey the gospel message to Felix, Festus, and King Agrippa, and perhaps even to Caesar himself.

Paul had many interests and was highly skilled and educated. His skill focus, however, was quite simple. Whether in written or spoken form, he wanted to be effectively communicating the gospel. The contexts varied widely, from riots in Jerusalem to a palace in Rome. The cultures he communicated in were also diverse. But the focus of his skill was very precise.

Developing skill requires an exceptionally focused sense of what I do.

CHAPTER FOUR

# *Skill and Success*

There are many stories of skillful men who zoom up the career ladder of success. Those men live in the books of the Bible and on the pages of the *Wall Street Journal.* It makes sense to us when skill and success end up partnering with each other.

Then there are the cases where men of mediocre skill face career stall-outs. Someone else is promoted, positions are eliminated, and functions are outsourced. Again, we can understand that scenario. It can be explained and understood.

But then there are other accounts, stories that also appear in Scripture and in the lives of men we all know. Sometimes men of genuine skill do not live in the glow of a successful career. What their skill ought to deliver somehow eludes them. They work hard and well, and little career good happens. That is not an uncommon happening.

We need to make one more point before we draw our study of skill to a conclusion:

**Working skillfully does not guarantee success.**

If David had written a resume, this is what it would have looked like on his thirtieth birthday:

David, son of Jesse

120 Goliath Falls Trail

Jerusalem, Israel

### BIOGRAPHICAL DATA

Born in Bethlehem to Jesse as the youngest of eight children. Married to Michal, daughter of Saul, king of Israel.

### WORK EXPERIENCE

*Shepherd;* Bethlehem

Responsibilities included taking care of my father's sheep and rescuing sheep from jaws of lions and bears. I also wrestled with lions and bears and killed them. Anointed king of Israel by Samuel the prophet.

*Musician to the royal court;* Jerusalem
Responsibilities included playing the harp for King Saul, especially when he was under significant pressure. Began part-time; went to full-time employment at the king's specific request.

*Shepherd, messenger;* Socoh in Judah and Bethlehem
Responsibilities included taking care of my father's sheep, as well as carrying messages and supplies to and from my father in Bethlehem and brothers fighting the Philistines under the command of King Saul. Accomplishments included killing the Philistine giant Goliath, who had defied both the Israelite army and God.

*High-ranking army officer, musician to the royal court;* Jerusalem
Responsibilities included playing the harp for King Saul when depressed. Also led military campaigns against the various enemies of Israel. Accomplishments included moving quickly up in rank as I led the troops successfully through many battles. Won constant recognition from fellow officers and soldiers, as well as the general public. Was

credited with more success than all the rest of Saul's officers. Reason for leaving: philosophical differences with employer, King Saul.

**REFERENCES**

Jonathan, son of Saul, king of Israel
Samuel, prophet of God

Notice the pattern evidenced by David's resume. He began in a relatively humble position as a shepherd, worked slowly into a significant job in the king's court, and shot to top of the mountain. What the resume fails to mention is that he soon fell off a cliff. Just when he was supposed to be getting into the stride of his career, near his thirtieth birthday, he became a fugitive running from the death penalty.

A more forthcoming resume would have included this entry:

*Fugitive;* Judah and Philistine
Responsibilities included trying to stay alive on the run while being pursued by King Saul and his army. Spent years camping out in the wilderness and living in caves. Supported myself by organizing raiding parties against Philistines, while at

other times joining the Philistines in raids against their enemies.

According to the text, David was very skilled at what he did. Furthermore, we know beyond a shadow of a doubt that he was called and anointed to be king of Israel. However in the middle of that calling and in the center of that evidence skill, he experienced anything but career success.

We need to be cautioned against thinking that if we perform our job skillfully we will automatically experience career success. Scripture makes no such promise. Many other things come into play as God fulfills His purpose and as we live out our calling. Success as the world defines it may or may not be one of the results. That, however, does not diminish our need and responsibility to perform our work with a high level of skill. God's definition of skill is still true and is still relevant even if it does not guarantee our career success.

## CHAPTER FIVE

# *What Skill Looks Like*

We are committed in this short series to offering real-life examples of the topic under discussion and scrutiny. In this chapter you will meet three men who live out what it means to be a skilled worker. They come from different walks of life.

Mickey Rapier is a musician and worship leader at Fellowship Bible Church in northwest Arkansas. He is one of our pastors and an exceptionally gifted man.

Ken Larson is the CEO of Slumberland, a chain of home-furnishings stores in the Midwest that is headquartered in St. Paul, Minnesota. We have always thought of Ken as an extraordinary entrepreneur.

Fitz Hill is a coach for the Arkansas Razorbacks.

### *The worship leader: Mickey Rapier*

Mickey Rapier isn't the type to live in clutter, so he keeps the closet door closed. This otherwise highly organized worship pastor doesn't use a computer or even a filing cabinet to compartmentalize the thousands of items he has collected for possible use during a Sunday service.

Instead, he uses the closet. Behind its closed door is the world of Mickey Rapier—stacks and stacks of music, notes, letters, and articles; anything he has come across and thought someday might apply to some message. There is a stack for Christmas and a stack for Easter. There are stacks for just about every other holiday or topic that might come up, and each stack grows by the day.

But the stacks are more than a practical mechanism for storing information. They are symbolic as well. They represent the core method Mickey uses to take his God-given talents and turn them into "creations of wonder and excellence." They represent how Mickey attacks every task he values—with a passion for learning as much as he can even if he might never use 99 percent of what he comes to know.

Mickey realized as a high school student that his passion for music and singing wouldn't develop without training, which he couldn't get in his rural community. But he wanted to sing. Ever since he heard the visiting music leader at his church's revival meeting, Mickey knew he wanted to sing. And it was beginning to dawn on him that singing was something he could give to God. He loved the competition of athletics, but he knew he could never play college ball, much less make a living in sports. He decided to sing for a living and use his gift for God.

But as a high school senior, he wasn't ready for Nashville, and he knew it. So he went to college on scholarship as a tuba player. And after overcoming an initial fear of performing before the university faculty, he earned a scholarship as a vocalist.

The more his teachers helped him develop his particular talents as a singer—primarily a French baritone voice that is as rich and delightful as your favorite hot-fudge dessert—the more he was eager to spend time practicing the craft. And the more he worked on his musical skills, the more he came to appreciate the skills of others. Even though he knew he would never sing opera, he wanted to study it. And the same held true for most other styles.

He began to study anything he could find about musicians, songwriters, and singers, with a particular leaning toward finding out what people were thinking when they wrote their songs. He was searching for the meaning, good or bad, behind the words and notes.

Mickey was also (and is) a student of people as well as words. He soaks in everything he sees in others. When they succeed, he wants to know why so he can imitate their methods. When they fail, he wants to know what went wrong so he can avoid it or correct it if he is ever in a similar situation. In college, he directed a small ensemble that traveled from church to church singing and sharing testimonies. He fell in love with the girl who would become his wife and the thrill of seeing people respond to the gospel.

His first church job was a part-time position he held while still in college. The senior pastor was a true shepherd to the people of his congregation, and he worked tirelessly and self-lessly to meet their needs. From him, Mickey began to refine his work ethic.

After leaving college, Mickey was full of energy and ready to set the world ablaze—starting with his first church—with new ideas. But the senior pastor there helped him harness that passion with patience, and Mickey came to understand the value of taking baby steps when those around him weren't ready to run.

His creative skills were developed largely at his next stop, a small church where the pastor had been a seventeen-year missionary to Japan. The pastor's time abroad made him open to new ideas, and he encouraged Mickey to be creative when organizing the services. When Mickey had a new idea, this pastor's response would be "Go for it." Once again, Mickey found himself deep in study, reading and listening to as much as possible in hopes of finding the perfect song or anecdote to fit the topic of the pastor's upcoming sermon. And with this pastor, a whole new world of modern Christian music was available to go along with the classics.

Mickey's next assignment was as leader of the college ministry in a large church near the campus of a state university. There his skills for administration were refined. No longer was he working with a congregation of two hundred, but a student population of twice that. He soon learned to "think big" and to delegate tasks to others either because they were better at those tasks or because he simply didn't have time to do it all. Administrative skills, which aptitude tests would later reveal he possessed, suddenly began to take shape.

Each stop along the way helped prepare Mickey for his current job as worship leader at a large regional church, where he is in charge of organizing and planning each week's worship celebration so that the songs, the teaching, the music, and all of the other tools he can come up with work together to drive home the theme of the day.

There is one other factor Mickey uses in developing the skills he needs for that job, one that works together with the self-study, the study of others, and the practice of mentoring. He calls it "the train wreck" factor. Every time Mickey wrecks the train—and sometimes he's the only one who notices that it has derailed—he finds something that makes future rides smoother. Each trip to the stage teaches something new about what audiences will respond to and what turns them off.

It is really trial and error. But it is trial and error with a focus. There is a point to the weeks upon weeks of planning with his staff, to the days upon days of practicing and memorizing, to the nights upon nights of reading, to the hours upon hours of listening to new music, and to the endless creative leaps he and his worship team take in front of thousands of worshipers.

It all fits with Mickey's passion for worship and his calling from God. And it gives him something to do with all the stuff in his closet.

### The entrepreneur: Ken Larson

Ken Larson was busy turning a small bedding company into a regional home-furnishings giant when he learned a huge lesson about motives.

A manufacturer had called one day to say that it was yielding to pressure from one of Ken's competitors and that Ken's Slumberland stores could no longer sell its product line.

So after a great deal of thought and consultation with friends, Ken decided to take legal action against both the competitor and the manufacturer. It was the right thing to do, he decided, and he was doing it for all the right reasons.

The system soon bore that out. Before the matter got to court, both parties agreed to settle. So Ken was feeling pretty good as he sat down in his attorney's office to sign the victory papers. But there was one paper Ken didn't count on signing—a confidentiality agreement.

Ken was devastated. He never thought he would have to sign something agreeing to keep the terms of the settlement a secret. But when that document was placed in front of him, Ken immediately came face-to-face with one of his primary motives behind taking the problem into the legal system. He wanted the community and the industry to know he had won. And the fact that he was in the right was more coincidental than he wanted to admit.

What God taught Ken that day was the importance of truly understanding his real motives. It has been an ongoing and difficult learning process for Ken, and he doesn't always like the answers he finds. But he strongly believes that once he understands his real motives, he has a much better chance of getting done what he wants to get done. And ultimately, the motives are more important to God than the numbers in a bank account.

Why is that relevant to developing skill? Understanding what motivates himself and those around him has been a key skill in Ken's success as an entrepreneur. It has been a central factor in his ability to build a home-furnishing empire that has grown to forty-six franchises and corporate stores in six different states.

There are other skills, of course, necessary to become a successful businessman. For Ken, some of the skill sets have changed as he has matured. Others have remained constant. The skills Ken finds important include:

• The ability to transition from one season of life to another. Ken isn't the same person he was fifteen or twenty years ago, and neither is his job. He went from being a manager who did everything to becoming a manager who delegated to others to becoming a CEO. The ability to adapt to the changes in his own personality, to the changes in his corporate world, and to the changes in his industry not only has helped keep Ken's company from growing stale, it's kept it on the cutting edge.

• The ability to trust and show confidence in those around you. Even though Ken has hundreds of employees, his day-to-day work requires him to relate to a relatively small group of key people. Those people must know Ken believes in them. It is something he can't fake. They know when he's not buying what they are selling or when he is losing confidence.

• The ability to listen and understand what others are communicating. Ken can't just sit quietly and nod his head when employees, customers, and vendors talk. He has to honestly understand what they mean in order to make the most of the information they have.

• The ability to value other people. As a matter of policy, Slumberland values other people. It is the VOP (Value of the Person) policy, and it starts at the top. Ken believes everyone in the company, from the top to the bottom, must show love, dignity, and respect for customers and coworkers.

• The ability to hire motivated people and then to keep them motivated. One of the ways he does that is with a psychological assessment. Every potential manager takes the test so that Ken will have an idea about what motivates the person, what the person's interest in the company is, and how the person will fit into the company culture.

The thread that runs through the entire fabric, though, is motivation—the empowering force that is derived from one's motives. Ken believes the key to success in any line of work is the ability to sell ideas. And the key to selling anything is motivation.

Developing such motivation from within requires more than coming up with ideas, but that is the first step. It requires developing a clear picture of what needs to be achieved. And for a leader of a company, it requires effectively translating those goals to a broader group of people.

Motivation is what separates the daydreamers from the achievers. It is the action screaming out more loudly than the words.

Defining a goal isn't always easy, but Ken has come to understand that there has to be a target. That target can change when circumstances change, but it can't fade away. When an employee loses sight of the target, his motivation soon disappears as well. People with nothing to shoot for seldom hit anything of value. That is why Ken believes the most powerful combination in an employee is when the individual's personal objective lines up with the corporate objective.

### *The coach: Fitz Hill*

Fitz Hill was in junior high school when he began refining the primary skill he would need for his career, even though he had no idea what he would do with his life or that what he was doing at the time would help make him good at it.

In fact, the skill Fitz Hill began learning then, and cherishes so dearly now, probably isn't one most people would associate with Hill's job as an assistant football coach at the University of Arkansas.

Football coaches are part salesman, part tactician, part teacher. To succeed, they must develop the ability to recruit and motivate good players. They must develop the ability to create a winning game plan. And they must develop the ability to train the members on the team.

They work twelve to fifteen hours a day during the season, watching film to find the smallest of weaknesses in their opponents, calling prospects who may never even visit the campus, much less play for the team, meeting with other members of the staff, meeting with the players, and, eventually, coaching the players.

But to Hill, those are all secondary skills.

The primary skill, the one that has become part of his second nature and the one that weaves its way through all the others, is the skill of influence.

The world, including his employers, may measure Hill's performance based on how many passes the receivers catch, how many touchdowns the offense scores, and how many wins the team posts. But Hill's measuring stick has one primary mark: how many lives he influences.

For Hill, the only thing he can take with him when he dies is his influence.

So while Hill was thrilled to see J. J. Meadors become the school's all-time leading receiver, he was more elated when Meadors phoned a year later to say he had completed his degree and gotten a job.

Hill had developed a relationship and made an impact.

Hill began learning his people skills when he was running for school offices. From the eighth grade through his senior year, Hill was elected president of either the student body or the student council.

It wasn't an easy task for an African American in a school that was 70 percent white. Hill knew he had to get the white vote without losing the African American vote. He needed friends from both races, so he began developing relationships.

But he had no idea he would be using those skills as a football coach. Hill played football in college, but he planned to be a journalist. He was working on those skills at Ouachita Baptist University when a family crisis changed his career track. Six weeks after his father lost a three-year-long battle with cancer, Hill's mother had a stroke that left her requiring twenty-four-hour care (to this day). Hill lived at home, cared for his mother, played football, and went to college for a semester until an aunt in California agreed to take in his mother.

It was during a 1984 Christmas trip to California to see his mother that Hill popped a cassette tape into his car stereo. He wasn't really interested in the tape, but a friend had given it to him. What else was he going to listen to while driving across the desert? So Hill listened as Grant Taft, then the head football coach at Baylor University, talked about coaching.

"Preachers, teachers, bankers—they have influence on people," Taft said. "But nobody has influence on people like a coach. A coach gets a kid's attention."

On that drive across the desert, Hill discovered his calling. He wanted to have the type of positive influence on kids that his parents had had on him. So instead of writing for the college newspaper, he spent his final two years of college writing head coaches all across the country in search of a job as a graduate assistant coach. He landed a spot at Northwestern (La.) State, then at Arkansas. The job at Arkansas soon turned into a full-time position.

Now Hill is busy coaching—and influencing.

When he first began coaching, Hill realized the true impact he could have on young athletes, especially other African Americans. Anything he told them to do, they did. He had a position of authority, and they immediately respected the position. The more time he spent around them, the more they learned to respect him as a person.

Hill was grateful for the twenty years he had had his parents, and he realized most of the African American kids he was coaching didn't have the advantage of such a strong and stable family. He was determined to fill in the gaps. So he began working on ways to develop trust and build relationships.

The political skills he learned early on were good, but he needed more. Hill has taken several approaches to refining his skills so that he can effectively lead young men.

For starters, he works hard to be sensitive to the needs of minorities. When he travels around the country to recruit players, be it the inner city or rural farmland, he really checks out the surroundings and tries to put himself in that environment. Hill comes from a good family and a good home, and now he makes a good living. But he refuses to look down on anyone who has less. He keeps in mind that our experiences shape our perspectives, and he tries to understand the perspectives of the young people he is contacting.

Hill likes to think of it as a camera lens. "Too many people," he says, "won't take the time to change the lens and look at things differently."

The older he gets, the more Hill has to work at learning and understanding what he sees when he switches to the lens of an eighteen-year-old. He works on that by staying in touch. In the off-season, when he doesn't have to yell and scream at his players, he invites them to his home for regular visits, and he drops by the apartment complex where most of the players live at least twice a week.

He listens to their music and watches their television shows, even when he doesn't always care for what he is hearing or seeing. And he listens closely to whatever they have to say.

When Hill was still a graduate assistant, his National Guard army-reserve unit was called to duty in Desert Storm. Hill's understanding of trust was heightened. Once the troops developed a trust in their leader, they were willing to die for him—just like Jesus died for us. Only after developing that trust can the leader exert his influence. Hill tries to develop the trust with his players first so that he can be in a position to influence their lifestyles.

Hill also has continued his formal education. In earning his master's degree in student personnel services and in working on his doctorate in education leadership, Hill has taken fifteen hours in counseling courses so that he can better understand what he sees and hears when he deals with his athletes.

When he completes his doctorate, Hill could switch career paths and no doubt rise quickly into a position as an administrator in an ivory-tower school. But he has no desire to do that. He wants to stay in the trenches, dealing with kids and their problems. The way he sees it, being a coach at a major college opens doors for him—doors into the homes of young people and doors into the offices of people who can help make social changes. And his higher education will lend credibility to the programs and solutions he devises.

It is just one more step in improving the skill he first began to develop way back in the eighth grade—the skill of influence.

# *Conclusion*

How can we sum up?

We were not sure where this study of skill would take us when we began. We have learned much that we did not know before. We now understand that Scripture defines skill very specifically. And that God Himself cares about the level of skill that His children display in their work. That the Holy Spirit is integral to our developing skill in our work.

But at the end of the study we are left with one unescapable feeling that helps put it all in perspective. For the Christian, skillful work is a form of worship to God. The raw ability itself comes from Him. He is intimately involved in its maturity through the Holy Spirit. And He brings us opportunities for learning, education, and experience to fine-tune it even further.

Skill is worship, just like developing godly character, knowing and living our calling, and serving.

"Bless all his skills, O Lord, and be pleased with the work of his hands" (Deuteronomy 33:11).

# *Where Do I Go from Here?*

1. *Define your skill.*

   It is impossible to develop something that cannot be defined. We recommend that you actually write down, in a couple of sentences or a paragraph, what your skill is. Take your time and be precise.

2. *Determine a plan for developing it.*

   Developing skill is a process, not an event. In fact, it most likely is a lifelong quest. How will it be developed? What are the steps? If it is impossible to lay out the entire plan, what are the obvious next steps?

3. *Become very intentional in praying for it.*

   As is clear from this study, the Holy Spirit is absolutely crucial to our skill development. The skill that you carefully defined above needs to be offered back to God. It is He who gave it to you; it is on His behalf that you exercise it. Ask Him to help you develop and evidence it to its fullness.

# *Notes*

## Chapter One

1. Peter S. Greenberg, "Dead-on landing demand makes Hong Kong flight last wild ride," *Los Angeles Times Syndicate*, as reported in the *Arkansas Democrat-Gazette*, 26 January 1997.

## Chapter Two

1. William Barclay, *The Mind of Jesus* (New York: Harper & Row, 1960), p. 9.
2. Ibid.

If you liked this book and would like to know more about ᵀᴴᴱLife@WorkC℠ or Cornerstone, please call us at 1-800-739-7863.

Other ways to reach us:

> Mail:    Post Office Box 1928
>              Fayetteville, AR 72702
>
> Fax:     (501) 443-4125
>
> E-mail:  LifeWork@CornerstoneCo.com